# Meetings That Work

# Meetings That Work

Marlene Caroselli, Ed.D.

**SkillPath Publications, Inc.**
**Mission, KS**

Editor: Kelly Scanlon

Editorial Assistant: Virginia Crabtree

Cover Design: Diane Flynn

ISBN: 1-878542-24-9

Printed in the United States of America

# Contents

# 1

## Introduction

Momentous decisions are made at meetings, decisions that can affect organizations or nations or even the world. Just think about a meeting held in Williamsburg, Virginia, in 1774. At that meeting, George Washington openly discussed resisting British oppression by force. The rest is history, American history.

Your meetings may not focus on such revolutionary issues. But they are important, nonetheless, if only because corporate time and money are spent on them.

Whether you would like to improve the efficiency of the meetings you *attend* or the meetings you *conduct*, this is the book for you. In it, we will explore some of the common misconceptions about meetings and try to debunk them. We will also try to validate some of the positive notions you may have. Toward that end, we have printed quotes in large italic type throughout the book. As you read each quote, decide whether you reject or believe the position being cited.

*"Convenio;*

*ergo,*

*sum."*

*("I meet;*

*therefore,*

*I am.")*

The book is also designed to examine the measures that must be taken if meeting participants and meeting leaders are to optimize the meeting process. Good meetings do not just happen. They are the result of careful planning, attention to participant needs, and follow through. If organizations are serious about satisfying customers, engaging in excellent processes, and delivering quality products and services, they must also be serious about the meeting process.

This book offers an active, "hands-on" approach to improving your meetings. It is not a book that you can simply read and then file away on the shelf. It is a book to be used—intensively and extensively—to be of value.

To guide you through the book, we have built several recurring features into each chapter, including:

- Highlighted text.
- Figures.
- Summary grids.
- Worksheets.

*Highlighted text.* Several spiral notepads are printed throughout the book. The items listed on the pads are intended to function as "notes" that highlight the concepts, steps, or processes necessary for achieving "meetings that work."

1

*Figures.* The figures in each chapter are designed to visually illustrate concepts that have been presented.

*Summary grids.* The concepts presented in each chapter are summarized in a grid at the end of the chapter. Review these summary grids prior to each meeting that you conduct or attend.

*Worksheets.* The worksheets are intended as exercises through which you can enhance your understanding of the concepts we present. Most of the worksheets first require you to record your present meeting experiences as they relate to the topic under discussion. Then you are asked to formulate or consider solutions and alternatives based on information presented in the chapter. The rationale behind these worksheets is to get you to focus *now* on ways to improve your meetings.

In addition, you will find two appendices that reinforce the active, "hands-on" approach stressed throughout the book.

The checklists in Appendix A are designed as "ready references" to assist meeting leaders in preparing for meetings. Each checklist contains items that must be taken care of before a meeting is held. On the facing page of each checklist, make notes about the individual items as you attend to them (e.g., phone numbers, names of individuals responsible for setting up the meeting room, list of visuals/equipment needed, etc.).

Appendix B contains forms that allow both meeting leaders and participants to evaluate various aspects of the meetings they attend. These forms can be removed from the book, copied, and distributed at the end of your meetings. The feedback you gather should help you fine-tune your organization's meeting processes so that you can achieve the results you want and move your organization closer to fulfilling its mission. Talk about the questions and discuss your answers with colleagues or supervisors. Don't restrict your discussions to your own company: compare your answers to the answers your associates in other companies would give.

By the time you have completed this book, you should be better equipped to answer the following questions:

- What is the value of meetings?
- What is the cost of meetings?
- What are some common complaints about meetings?
- What are the types of meetings?
- What are the steps involved in some common problem-solving techniques?
- What is the "RE-7" approach to meetings?

Once you have worked through the book yourself, use it as a basis for training programs or lunchtime seminars.

Before you begin, however, take a few minutes to complete the following worksheet. It will help you focus on your past meeting experiences and on your current beliefs about what constitutes a good or a bad meeting. As you read through the book, notice whether you find those beliefs changing.

## ✍ Worksheet 1
### Focusing on Your Meeting Experiences

1.  Briefly, but specifically, describe the worst meeting you ever attended.

    _____

    _____

    _____

    _____

    _____

    _____

2.  Now describe the best meeting you ever attended.

    _____

    _____

    _____

    _____

    _____

    _____

    _____

3.  How would you describe the meetings you typically attend?

    _____

    _____

    _____

4.  How would you describe those you typically conduct?

    _____

    _____

    _____

    _____

# 2

## Meeting Basics: Addressing Some Common Misconceptions and Complaints

### The Value of Meetings

There are those who believe that productivity is predicated on meetings and others who believe that productivity is prevented by meetings. Between these two extremes are a host of other views concerning the worth, or value, of meetings. The most prevalent opinion seems to be that meetings waste time. Meetings are expensive; there is no doubt about it. But, the expenditure of time, effort, and money can be worthwhile if those involved take advantage of the opportunities meetings afford. Figure 1 summarizes the opportunities available to those involved in meetings.

A well-organized, well-run meeting can *save* time and increase productivity by bringing together a group of people intent on exchanging information that can move the organization forward. Meetings are the most efficient means for ensuring that every person in the organization is kept abreast of vital information. Positive results can be achieved regularly if the meeting process is measured and continuously improved.

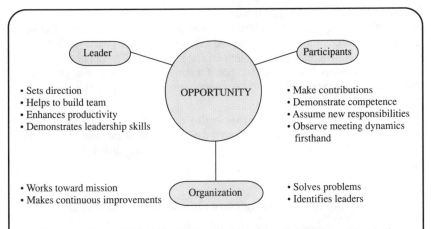

**Fig. 1.** If well-organized and well-run, meetings provide opportunities for all involved.

## The Cost of Meetings

*"America leads the world not in steel or textile but in meetings. The problem is, how do you export meetings?"*

**— Robert Half**

Because American business people spend so much time in meetings, it behooves us to maximize what is accomplished during those meetings. If meeting time is well spent, the value of meetings can outweigh their cost.

Consider these data:

- The Wharton Center for Applied Research found that, excluding preparation time, senior executives spend 23 hours a week in meetings but consider only 58% of that time effectively spent.

- The accounting firm of Laventhol and Horwath learned that more than $41 billion is spent each year on corporate and association conferences (including travel and lodging).

- Goodrich and Sherwood, a New York City human relations consulting firm, studied 100 executives who revealed that more than one-third of their time is spent in meetings.

- Burket Marketing Research reports that an executive who earns $50,000 a year earns $20,621 of that amount sitting in meetings, one-third of which he or she considers unnecessary. (In total, those "unnecessary" meetings consume six weeks of the executive's working year.)

- Five executives who earn $40,000 a year and who meet for one hour each week cost their firm nearly $200 for that hour when all costs are added in (fringe benefits, preparation time, and meeting materials). That figure translates to nearly $10,000 in a given year.

### Common Complaints About Meetings

Some of the most common complaints about meetings as well as some of the major reasons for their costliness revolve around the meeting process itself—it is a *process*, after all, one that can be examined and improved. If complaints can be identified and reduced or eliminated, then it naturally follows that your meetings will be less costly. Some of the most common complaints are listed on the next page.

A successful and efficiently conducted meeting can produce *measurable*, as well as *immeasurable,* savings in terms of improved morale, motivation, and so forth. The goal of all meetings is to ensure that all who attend feel their time is well-spent.

*"A manager spending more than 25 percent of time in meetings is a sign of malorganization."*

**— Peter Drucker**

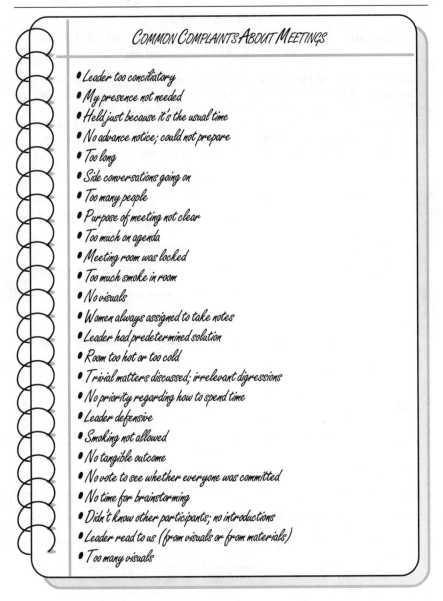

## COMMON COMPLAINTS ABOUT MEETINGS

- Leader too conciliatory
- My presence not needed
- Held just because it's the usual time
- No advance notice; could not prepare
- Too long
- Side conversations going on
- Too many people
- Purpose of meeting not clear
- Too much on agenda
- Meeting room was locked
- Too much smoke in room
- No visuals
- Women always assigned to take notes
- Leader had predetermined solution
- Room too hot or too cold
- Trivial matters discussed; irrelevant digressions
- No priority regarding how to spend time
- Leader defensive
- Smoking not allowed
- No tangible outcome
- No vote to see whether everyone was committed
- No time for brainstorming
- Didn't know other participants; no introductions
- Leader read to us (from visuals or from materials)
- Too many visuals

*"If an hour has been spent amending a sentence,*
*someone will move to delete the paragraph."*
**— Anonymous**

### ✍ Worksheet 2
## Remedies for Reducing Complaints About and the Cost of Meetings in My Organization

In what ways do you feel money is being wasted in your organization as far as meetings are concerned? Select from the list of common meeting complaints the ten you feel are most responsible for meetings that fail. Rank your complaints on a scale of 1 to 10, with "1" being your choice for the primary cause of nonproductive meetings. Then record the actions you feel you can take to ensure that these offending situations occur less often.

_____

_____

_____

_____

_____

_____

_____

_____

_____

_____

_____

_____

_____

_____

_____

_____

_____

_____

_____

_____

## Types of Meetings

While the reasons people meet are varied, meetings generally fall into three broad categories:

*"A meeting is an activity engaged in by a group that takes minutes but wastes hours."*

— **Anonymous**

- Information-giving
- Information-exchanging
- Information-creating

Several different types of meetings can be subsumed within each of these categories, as shown below.

*Information-giving* meetings are typically one-way meetings. When the meeting leader has information to disseminate rather than ideas to discuss, he or she will often hold a meeting and simply deliver the message. This type of meeting is suited for any size group and is especially ideal for large groups. Because the object is to deliver information quickly, the meeting is often formal and businesslike. Such meetings can be held to:

- Train.
- Introduce a new concept, product, or person.
- Motivate.
- Persuade.
- Demonstrate a system.
- Delegate.
- Quell rumors or relieve tension.
- Gain support for an idea or product.

*Information-exchanging* meetings are called in order to exchange ideas. Two-way communication is encouraged to enable the sender and the receiver to exchange roles and to benefit from listening to one another's ideas, thus clarifying and refining the message. These types of meetings work best when attendance is limited to around thirty individuals. Due to their nature—the exchange of information—these meetings are usually less formal than information-giving meetings. These meetings provide opportunities to:

- Conduct one-on-one exchanges such as performance interviews.
- Socialize.
- Garner support for a decision or approach.
- Hear staff reports.
- Exchange ideas within an interest group.
- Reconcile opposing views.

*Information-creating* meetings depend on the creativity of the participants and the unleashing of original ideas important for planning and problem solving. These meetings work best with small groups of individuals who can offer relaxed, spontaneous responses. These meetings are called to:

- Make decisions.
- Solve problems.
- Analyze situations.
- Formulate goals.
- Move along the efforts of a task force (which disbands once the task is accomplished).
- Create or develop ideas through brainstorming.
- Actually work as a group (e.g., to develop a position paper or engage in planning).
- Discuss ideas.

## Communication Styles

The three basic types of meetings can be related to the three styles of communicating:

- Bull's-eye style
- Ping-pong style
- Spiral style

**Fig. 2.** The bull's-eye style of communicating mirrors the information-giving approach to meetings.

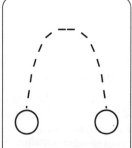

**Fig. 3.** The ping-pong style of communicating involves an exchange or sharing of ideas.

**Fig. 4.** The spiral style of communicating is used to reshape ideas in information-creating meetings.

### Bull's-Eye Style
The bull's-eye style is essentially an information-giving approach (Fig. 2). The sender of the information is concerned with delivering a specific message. If the message hits the intended mark, the sender is satisfied. The sender is not especially concerned with obtaining feedback from listeners or readers; he or she is only concerned with conveying a message.

### Ping-Pong Style
A communicator who uses the ping-pong style *is* concerned with the questions or responses the receiver may have. The communicator has a message to deliver, but

the success of that delivery is at least partially dependent on the understanding of the listener or reader. Too, the message may be further shaped or defined by the responses the recipient provides. This style of communication is often used in information-sharing meetings (Fig. 3).

### Spiral Style

The spiral style does not represent a complete communication transaction. Rather, the communicator sends a message and engages the recipients in an ongoing consideration of the message and its numerous implications (Fig. 4). The sender of the message considers nuances, which may be as important as the original thought. Spiraling means reading between the lines and provoking new ideas related to the initial communication prompt, which is continuously being reshaped. The spiral style is common to information-creating meetings.

## The Problem-Solving Process

Often, information-sharing and information-creating meetings are called for the purpose of solving problems. For that reason, we are including some problem-solving techniques you may find useful.

Problem solving is best viewed as a process consisting of several steps. Each step helps the group clarify the problem and move closer toward a solution.

The steps in the problem-solving process are as follows:

1. Define the problem.
2. Analyze the problem.
3. Generate several possible solutions.
4. Select one solution and plan its implementation.
5. Implement the solution.
6. Evaluate the solution.

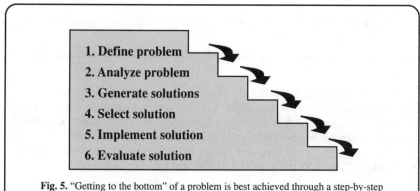

**1. Define problem**
**2. Analyze problem**
**3. Generate solutions**
**4. Select solution**
**5. Implement solution**
**6. Evaluate solution**

**Fig. 5.** "Getting to the bottom" of a problem is best achieved through a step-by-step approach that brings the problem and its solution(s) into focus.

## Problem-Solving Techniques

Two specific problem-solving techniques are described on the following pages: the fishbone technique and the brainstorming technique.

*The Fishbone Technique.* So-called because it resembles the skeletal outline of a fish, the fishbone problem-solving technique affords a rapid and thorough examination of several possible causes of a problem. Using a simple line diagram, the person or group trying to resolve the problem describes the nature of the problem. In a box representing the fish head, the problem is stated simply. To the left of the "fish head," the major causes of the problem are listed as "cause categories" beside each of the major "bone" lines in the skeleton. Possible reasons, or "subcauses," are listed along dotted horizontal lines.

For example, let us assume your problem is that you cannot find enough time to do all the work on your desk each day (Fig. 6). Write the problem in a box on the right-hand side of a sheet of paper. Next, draw the fishbone diagram, listing the major causes of the problem along the "bone" lines. (You may, of course, list as many causes as appropriate. In Figure 6, we mention the four "M" categories only because they are easy to remember.)

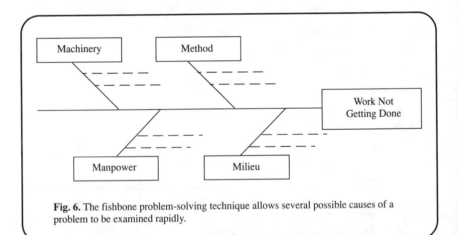

**Fig. 6.** The fishbone problem-solving technique allows several possible causes of a problem to be examined rapidly.

Then, on the horizontal lines adjacent to each cause category line, list the underlying causes. For example, under "milieu," you may list some ways in which the milieu, or environment, is preventing work from being done: too much noise, cigarette smoke causing headaches, too many telephone interruptions, and so forth. Next, examine these possible causes and decide which one is most likely causing the problem. Then work on ways to deal with that cause or causes.

*The Brainstorming Technique.* The brainstorming technique is popular, perhaps because it is so easy to use and is a quick way to generate ideas in a short period of time. The brainstorming "rules" are few and simple, but they must be adhered to if the technique is to be effective.

Before you begin, make certain everyone understands the problem in the same way. Write the problem and post it so all can see.

Once the idea-generation stage has begun, do not censure any idea that is given; record all that are suggested. Work quickly without discussing ideas.

Once the idea-generating stage is complete, evaluate the worth of each solution and pursue those that seem most promising. If you are in charge of planning a meeting, you may wish to use the brainstorming approach to help you decide which items would be most useful to include on the agenda or to determine in advance which committees should be formed, what assignments should be given, and so forth.

## Brainstorming "Rules"

**Before Beginning:**

• Ensure that everyone understands the problem.

**Idea-Generation Stage:**

• Do not dismiss any ideas; record them all.
• Work quickly; don't discuss ideas.

**Evaluation Stage:**

• Evaluate each idea.
• Pursue those that are most relevant.

## ✍ Worksheet 3
## Reconciling Differences Through
## the Problem-Solving Process

Answer the questions below regarding your opinion and your supervisor's opinion of the meetings in your organization. If the opinions differ, use one of the problem-solving techniques described in this chapter to reconcile your differences.

My feelings about the meetings I attend:

_____

_____

_____

_____

_____

My supervisor's feelings about the meetings I attend:

_____

_____

_____

_____

If these two points of view diverge, what can you do to reconcile the differences?

_____

_____

_____

_____

## Summary

The following grid summarizes the characteristics of the three types of meetings described in this chapter, including the communication styles and problem-solving techniques appropriate to each type. Deciding beforehand which type of meeting to hold will help you plan your meeting more effectively, thereby making it more productive. And, as we have discussed, a well-planned, productive meeting actually *saves* time and money.

| Characteristic | TYPE OF MEETING | | |
| --- | --- | --- | --- |
| | Information-Giving | Information-Sharing | Information-Creating |
| Purpose | Convey information | Create dialogue; exchange ideas | Find new solutions |
| Size | Any size; ideal for large groups | From 2 to 30 people is ideal | Best with small groups |
| Tone | Formal, businesslike | Usually less formal | Relaxed, spontaneous |
| Communication Style | Bull's-Eye | Ping-Pong | Spiral |
| Problem-Solving Technique | Any can be used, but formal problem-solving process is most common; problem-solving is completed before the meeting is called | Any process | Any process |

*"A meeting is one of the best postgraduate courses you can take."*
**— Bert Auger**

# 3

## Leader and Participant Behaviors That Contribute to Successful Meetings

Successful, productive meetings do not just happen. They depend on the behaviors of both the meeting leader and the meeting participants. In this chapter, we will discuss (1) some of the traits that allow a meeting leader to be a *facilitator*, a leader that keeps a meeting moving toward its goals, and (2) participant behaviors that contribute to successful meetings. As you proceed through the chapter, you will be presented with worksheets giving you an opportunity to evaluate your own meeting behavior as well as that of others you attend meetings with.

## Profile of a Successful Meeting Leader

### Leadership Styles

Leadership can be viewed as a continuum, ranging from an authoritative style at one end to a much more relaxed style at the other (Fig. 7). Between is a style that combines the best elements of both extremes. Each of us falls somewhere on this continuum.

At one end, is the *autocratic* leader who takes charge of every aspect of a project. The autocratic leader is always in control, enjoys exercising power, and is able to achieve a great deal because he or she organizes and follows through on all phases of the work. Subordinates usually respect the efficiency of this leader's style, which works best with employees who are relatively new at their jobs.

At the other end of the continuum is the *laissez-faire* leader. Laissez-faire is a French term meaning "allow [others] to do" what they think is best. The leader utilizing a laissez-faire style keeps his or her direction to a minimum, stepping in only when necessary for maintaining order. Such a style is ideal when employees have been with the company for a long time and have demonstrated their expertise and trustworthiness.

In the middle is the *democratic* leader. (This style is also described as "partici-pative.") This leader maintains *ultimate* control of the group's decisions and actions but encourages group members to contribute ideas and expertise so that the course of action is one that all, or most, have agreed to. The democratic leader encourages group member's participation in issues that involve them and listens carefully to ideas. Sometimes he or she will even become a one-person/one-vote member of the group, allowing the majority rule (not his or her own) to determine the course of action.

In Figure 7, place an "X" to indicate where you think *your* leadership style falls on the continuum.

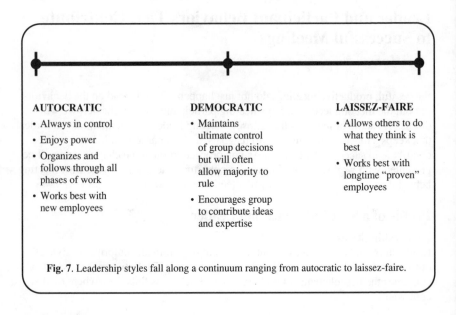

**AUTOCRATIC**
- Always in control
- Enjoys power
- Organizes and follows through all phases of work
- Works best with new employees

**DEMOCRATIC**
- Maintains ultimate control of group decisions but will often allow majority to rule
- Encourages group to contribute ideas and expertise

**LAISSEZ-FAIRE**
- Allows others to do what they think is best
- Works best with longtime "proven" employees

**Fig. 7**. Leadership styles fall along a continuum ranging from autocratic to laissez-faire.

## Traits and Skills

No matter which leadership style a meeting leader embraces, every *good* meeting leader must possess certain traits and skills that enable him or her to conduct a successful meeting. Mastering these skills can advance a career. The inability to do so, however, can damage a career. Among other things, a meeting leader should be:

- Analytical.
- Impersonal.
- A quick thinker.
- A clear communicator.
- Unbiased.
- Patient.
- Able to keep a group on target.
- Tactful.
- Cool under pressure.
- Restrained.
- Able to see the humor in situations.

## ✍ Worksheet 4
## Traits or Skills a Meeting Leader Should Possess

Think of the best leader you have ever known and then list the traits that person possessed. Think too about the types of skills (e.g., conflict resolution) that leaders are called upon to display—skills that can advance or damage a career.

_____

_____

_____

_____

_____

_____

_____

_____

_____

_____

_____

_____

_____

_____

_____

_____

_____

_____

_____

_____

## Positive Leader Behaviors

Some of the positive behaviors a meeting leader can exhibit are described in the following paragraphs. As you read through them, consider which of the behaviors contribute most to successful meetings. Which behaviors do you exhibit as a meeting leader?

Support group members and endeavors by being open and encouraging. Attempt to obtain input from all participants. Don't use your authority as meeting leader to interrupt others or to be harsh in your criticism. Meetings should not be used as a time for reprimanding others.

Serve as a catalyst by posing questions or proposing ideas for the group to contemplate. Stimulate the group's thinking by being clear in your directions and commentary. Offer guidance when the discussion lags, but refrain from controlling every phase of the meeting. Turn the meeting over to other appropriate leaders.

*"In a staff meeting, the supervisor is a leader, observer, expediter, questioner, and decision-maker. Please note that the role of lecturer is not listed. A supervisor should never use staff meetings to pontificate."*
— **Andrew S. Grove**

Maintain the harmony by stepping in if two members seriously disagree with one another. You might suggest that they take their dispute to another room and come back to the group with a resolution. Or, lighten a tense atmosphere with humor. You might get the group's attention and then announce that you want to postpone the issue until everyone has had an opportunity to study it further. You might even call for a break, just to give the disputants a chance to calm down. Of course, if you are able to anticipate an altercation, you might wish to meet with the likely combatants ahead of time and ask for their cooperation.

*"The executive has not yet been born who will concede that he, personally, is a bust at meetings; that he himself has ever lost control of a group or, worse, wasted time at somebody else's meeting by rambling on and on, entranced by the music of his own voice."*
— **Herbert Mayer**

As a facilitator, remind participants at least once during the meeting of the shared goal and/or proper meeting behaviors.

Don't ramble and don't permit others to do so.

If necessary, garner support for your position *before* the meeting begins.

Try to achieve consensus on each issue as it is discussed, before moving to the next item on the agenda.

If you are controlling more than fifty percent of the meeting, you probably should not be having the meeting. Situations that primarily involve one-way communication can often be handled in a written format such as a memo or a bulletin board announcement.

Take notes on *all* that occurs during the meeting, not only on issues that are being discussed and decisions that are being made, but also on how the participants are relating to one another, who is making especially salient remarks, who is dominating the meeting, and so forth.

These notes should be your personal account of the meeting, observations you can use as a basis for improving future meetings. Do not confuse these notes with the minutes of the meeting. As we will discuss in Chapter 4, the minute-taker is responsible for creating the official record of the meeting's proceedings.

Try to use and to elicit "we" behaviors and speech patterns, as opposed to the dominating "I" or the accusatory "you" attitudes.

As the meeting leader, you still have options if no concurrence is reached on an issue:

- Appoint a special task force to investigate alternate choices and to report at the next meeting.
- Ask a higher authority to make a ruling.
- Adjourn the meeting and give others an opportunity to consider the situation further.
- Vote and let the majority rule.
- Have the most vocal objectors state their specific oppositions and see if compromise can be reached on each of the points.
- Schedule a guest speaker at the next meeting who can give empirical data to support one point of view or the other.
- Have others submit their vote to you in writing (with a rationale for their decision) within the next week.
- Seek a compromise. For example, try one option for a week and see how it works before deciding to accept or reject it altogether.
- Suggest a totally different possibility, eliminating the two that are causing the conflict.

Take several copies of the Leader Evaluation Form in Appendix B to your next meeting. If you are actually the meeting leader, distribute the forms and use the feedback you obtain to improve your performance at the next meeting. If you are not the leader, encourage the leader to distribute the forms to measure his or her effectiveness.

## ✍ Worksheet 5
## Three Behaviors Most Important for
## Meeting Leaders to Display

Now that you have read through the descriptions of meeting leader behaviors, select the three you feel could most improve the flow of *your* next meeting.

1. Leader Behavior: _____

_____

_____

How It Could Be Implemented in My Organization: _____

_____

_____

2. Leader Behavior: _____

_____

_____

How It Could Be Implemented in My Organization: _____

_____

_____

3. Leader Behavior: _____

_____

_____

How It Could Be Implemented in My Organization: _____

_____

_____

_____

**Preparing for Difficult Situations**

As a meeting leader, you will be called on at times to use your traits and skills to handle difficult situations. Having the perfect comment available to use at these times will help you keep your meeting on target and ensure that you do not make inappropriate remarks. Ten common difficult situations are listed below.

## 10 Common Difficult Meeting Situations

- Latecomers
- Irrelevant, unworkable suggestions
- Good points not related to topic under discussion
- Attendees who don't contribute
- Attendees who ramble or overelaborate on every point
- Rude, mocking comments about suggested ideas
- Whispering or note writing among attendees
- Combative attitudes towards other participants
- Presenters who are not prepared
- Sexist comments

## ✍ Worksheet 6
## Preparing for Difficult Situations

Use the following space to record your *own* ideas for handling the difficult situations just discussed. You may wish to draw from previous experiences or to confer with a colleague as you prepare your statements. Practice the remarks until you can recall them quickly and they appear smooth and natural.

1. Someone who comes in late: _____

_____

2. Someone who makes an irrelevant, unworkable suggestion: _____

_____

3. Someone who makes a good point but one that is not related to the topic under discussion: _____

_____

4. Someone who does not contribute at all: _____

_____

5. Someone who rambles or overelaborates on every point: _____

_____

6. Someone who makes rude, mocking comments about something you, or someone else, says: _____

_____

7. Someone who whispers or writes notes to others throughout the meeting:

_____

8. Someone who attacks another person: _____

_____

9. Someone who makes a presentation for which he or she is clearly unprepared: _____

_____

10. Someone who makes a sexist comment: _____

_____

### Dealing With Participant Types

Certain types of people seem to appear at meetings throughout the land. These people are easy to recognize, for their behavioral patterns are quite distinct. Look over the following descriptions of meeting characters and *mentally* align some people you know or have known with each type listed. The leadership style you use and your mastery of specific leadership skills will play a major role in determining the types of contributions these individuals are capable of making.

Role-playing these situations with a colleague may help to reinforce your understanding of these types and how to deal with them.

*Always-Confused Type.* You may be tempted to think that the always-confused type is putting on an act—and you may be right! This sort of person sometimes views his or her behavior as eccentric or amusing. There are people who *always* misplace their car keys or constantly lose their gloves, scarves, and other items. They go into a mild panic, causing others to attend to them. In a meeting, such types appear disorganized, forgetful, and unprofessional. Their actions can waste valuable time.

*Clown Type.* The clown, like the always-confused type, feels a need to draw attention. Sometimes this person will play practical jokes; at other times, he or she will *tell* jokes. The clown is usually easier to tolerate than the always-confused type because he or she really is funny. And while a little levity will go a long way in alleviating the serious nature of most business meetings, the clown's behavior is often inappropriate or excessive.

*Attentive Type.* Since meetings are microcosms of a larger society, they typically contain the full spectrum of personality types, from the least desirable to the most productive. At the positive end of the spectrum is the attentive type, the person who listens carefully to all points of view, who takes notes, and who makes relevant comments. Such types are models who, ideally, will be imitated.

*Constant Complainer Type.* Sooner or later, you are bound to run into this type of meeting goer. The constant complainer has petty concerns and is so interested in voicing personal displeasure that he or she often cannot attend to the situation at hand. The constant complainer, if humored, will continue to take up time with matters that do not deserve the attention of the entire group. Gently, but firmly, the constant complainer must be told to focus on the subject under discussion.

*Creative Type.* The imaginative thinker makes a valuable contribution to any group but often fails to have a pragmatic approach for implementing the innovative ideas he or she seems to generate so easily. One way to channel the inventive energy of a creative type is to present him or her with the problem or meeting topic *before* the group assembles. Ask the person to come to the meeting with a prioritized list of suggestions. You can also team a creative type with a more pragmatic type to maximize the contributions of each.

*Devil's-Advocate Type.* This type of meeting attendee can play an important role. When the devil's advocate poses a question that seems to run contrary to accepted policies or plans, he or she may in fact be helping the group avoid "group think." (When groups engage in "group think," they do not allow opposing voices to share concerns.) So, the devil's advocate should be regarded as a valuable contributor: he or she is helping the meeting members to consider all sides of an issue instead of rushing into a decision prematurely.

*Doom-and-Gloom Type.* For whatever reason, certain people seem to take a perverse pleasure in presenting the negative point of view. Perhaps they are pessimistic by nature or perhaps they simply enjoy pricking the balloon of possibility, but they nonetheless are quick to point out all the reasons why a particular course of action is destined for failure. In dealing with doom-and-gloom types, it is necessary to keep a balanced perspective. Do not permit their negativity to destroy good ideas. On the other hand, don't reject their ideas completely. Sometimes their dire pronouncements make us more cautious. We should consider the predicted pitfalls, but we should be realistic in our considerations.

*Eager-Beaver Type.* The eager-beaver type is ready, willing, and usually able to assist with any undertaking, to join any committee, to do any task that needs to be done. The problem is that this type sometimes is overcommitted and, therefore, cannot complete assignments on time. The meeting leader should help guide this type of meeting participant to the activities that best utilize his or her talents.

*Easily-Offended Type.* Sensitive by nature, the easily-offended type may find insult where none was intended. As a meeting leader, or even as a meeting attendee, you will probably know about this personality quirk in advance of the meeting. But even if you do not have such insight, you must maintain control over the meeting. Keep attuned to the emotional climate. Do not permit altercations to erupt: defuse potentially volatile situations before they occur. Maintain your own emotional equilibrium and say or do nothing that might be interpreted as unkind.

*Hostile Type.* Some people are hostile by nature. Others may simply have had a rough day. Whatever the cause of the hostility you may encounter at meetings, there are ways for dealing with it professionally and evenly. If you are fairly certain that a hostile type will be attending an upcoming meeting and will "vent his spleen," schedule some time *before* the meeting so the two of you can thoroughly discuss the subject.

If hostility erupts during the meeting, give the hostile person an opportunity to express his or her point of view, but do not permit that person to dominate the meeting.

*Leader-of-the-Revolution Type.* This type of participant often feels a need to defy authority. The cause of the revolt may be less important to the person than the need to revolt, to draw attention, or to assert his or her leadership by acquiring followers at your expense. If possible, you should explore in advance such a participant's reaction to any ideas you intend to present at the meeting. Try to gain the person's support before the meeting begins. If the revolt catches you by surprise, however, you may have to postpone a decision about the issue(s) by suggesting that a committee meet to examine the objections further.

***Power-Seeker Type.*** The power seeker will attempt to acquire power in whatever way possible, including befriending the individuals he or she thinks have power or displaying knowledge that others do not possess. He or she may demonstrate power by engaging in office politics or by working against the system. In a myriad of ways, the power seeker will strive for self-aggrandizement. Often this type can be appeased by being given a project over which he or she can have control and through which he or she can accomplish a great deal for the organization.

***Nonstop-Talker Type.*** Such a person, no matter what his or her other attributes, can detract from the group's accomplishments with rambling, irrelevant discussions. A number of stop tactics are available for dealing with this type. The best idea is probably to have the meeting's time monitor objectively cut off anyone who goes beyond a two-minute discussion of any topic.

You might also announce at the beginning of the meeting that, in the interest of time, you would like to hold all discussion until after the major points have been presented. Or, you may appoint the nonstop talker to a position that requires him or her to stay busy taking notes or recording information on flip charts and so forth. Whatever tactic you employ, treat this type with consideration but be mindful of the group's needs as well.

***Show-Off Type.*** Usually the worst damage the show-off creates is to make others feel uncomfortable or even inadequate about their achievements compared to the show-off's own accomplishments. This type frequently does make a significant contribution to the organization but, in doing so, may annoy or alienate others. As a leader, you may wish to diplomatically discuss with the show-off the negative impact of such behavior on others. Acknowledge the show-off's talents, but ask the person to temper his or her display of them.

***Shy, Silent Type.*** Valuable ideas may remain unspoken by individuals who are shy or silent unless you make it a point to ask for their opinion. Some employees are naturally shy, reluctant to voice their ideas—either because they are uncomfortable being the center of attention or because they do not think their ideas merit the group's attention. The sensitive meeting leader will ensure that all members have been heard from.

***Supportive Type.*** Take advantage of this individual, especially if you think there will be opposition to an idea you would like to present at an upcoming meeting. The supportive type can be counted on to come to your defense if you need validation for a proposal or support for a plan. Such individuals often serve as peacemakers who share your vision or who understand your goals for the organization. These types are willing to speak up and help you win the group's support.

***Well-Prepared Type.*** Inevitably, some individuals will take the time to thoroughly research the agenda topics. These types are well-prepared no matter what the situation. Call upon these individuals when you have an especially complex or time-consuming item under consideration. Give them an opportunity to display their thoroughness and careful attention to detail. Such assignments benefit the well-prepared type, the meeting leader, the group, and the organization itself.

## ✍ Worksheet 7
## Suggestions for Dealing With Participant Types

Describe how you, as a meeting leader, can help each of the following types of participants maximize their contributions and, thus, optimize meeting circumstances.

1. Always-Confused Type: _____

_____

_____

2. Clown Type: _____

_____

_____

3. Attentive Type: _____

_____

_____

4. Constant Complainer Type: _____

_____

_____

5. Creative Type: _____

_____

_____

6. Devil's-Advocate Type: _____

_____

_____

7. Doom-and-Gloom Type: _____

_____

_____

8. Eager-Beaver Type: _____

_____

_____

9. Easily-Offended Type: _____

_____

_____

10. Hostile Type: _____

_____

_____

11. Leader-of-the-Revolution Type: _____

_____

_____

12. Power-Seeker Type: _____

_____

_____

13. Nonstop-Talker Type: _____

_____

_____

14. Show-Off Type: _____

_____

_____

15. Shy, Silent Type: _____

_____

_____

16. Supportive Type: _____

_____

_____

17. Well-Prepared Type: _____

_____

_____

## Profile of Successful Meeting Participants

Does your presence as a participant help make meetings sizzle, fizzle, or just plain drizzle? Consider your own meeting behaviors as you read through the positive participant behaviors described in the following paragraphs.

Commit to making the meeting worthwhile instead of complaining about it, thereby perpetuating the myth that meetings are a waste of time. Recognize that this conference may be an opportunity to gain visibility and to show others what you are capable of doing. Regard your attendance at the meeting as part of the work you are being paid to do.

*"One either meets or one works. One cannot do both at the same time."*

— **Peter Drucker**

Review the minutes of the last meeting and study the agenda ahead of time. Do your homework: review the issues and background material so you are prepared to participate in discussions. Formulate intelligent questions prior to attending. Assemble materials you will need to take. If you were given an action item during an earlier meeting, be certain it is done and done well.

Be on time.

Don't always sit with the same people, in the same place.

Demonstrate the "we" attitude. Volunteer for some of the tasks being assigned. Practice your listening skills; try not to interrupt. Be open to the ideas of others. Don't engage in side discussions and don't ramble when contributing to the main discussion.

Take notes and ask questions. If you note an error, speak up so it can be corrected.

Wait until others have had an opportunity to speak so you can get a feel for the issues and attitudes being conveyed. If, on the other hand, the leader has asked a question and no one is answering it, your effort to break a long silence will surely be appreciated.

Be prepared to defend your ideas.

If you are scheduled to make a presentation and are somewhat nervous about it, "plant" a colleague in the room (or in the audience). If you panic and forget what you are going to say next or if you are mercilessly challenged by someone else, the plant will ask you a prearranged question that you can easily answer. This little ploy will help restore your confidence so you can continue over the rough spot.

If the meeting does not remain on target and time runs out, suggest that the leader bring closure to the transaction under discussion. (The time monitor, of course, should be alert to such situations.) The closure may be in the form of a vote, a tabling of the discussion, or an appointment of one person to follow through on the point under consideration.

Present the meeting leader with an evaluation of the meeting he or she has just conducted. Include both positive and negative comments, if appropriate. The Meeting Observation Form in Appendix B is designed for such purposes.

## ✍ Worksheet 8
## Three Behaviors Most Important for
## Meeting Participants to Display

Describe the three participant behaviors you feel could most enhance your next meeting and discuss how each behavior can be implemented.

1. Participant Behavior: _____

_____

_____

_____

How This Could Be Implemented in My Organization: _____

_____

_____

_____

2. Participant Behavior: _____

_____

_____

_____

How This Could Be Implemented in My Organization: _____

_____

_____

_____

3. Participant Behavior: _____

_____

_____

How This Could Be Implemented in My Organization: _____

_____

_____

_____

## Summary

The following grid compares the meeting behaviors that leaders and participants demonstrate to achieve successful, productive meetings.

| COMPARISON OF LEADER AND PARTICIPANT BEHAVIORS ||
| --- | --- |
| **Leader** | **Participant** |
| Be open and encouraging. | Decide to make the meeting worthwhile. |
| Serve as a catalyst by posing questions. | Attempt to answer leader's questions, especially if a long silence has ensued. |
| Maintain harmony; remind participants of shared goals and appropriate meeting behaviors. | Defend your ideas, but exercise appropriate meeting behavior. |
| Don't ramble. | Don't ramble. |
| Gather support for ideas before the meeting. | Review minutes of last meeting; study agenda; assemble materials; complete tasks assigned at the last meeting. |
| Don't control or dominate the discussion. | Practice listening skills; don't engage in side discussions. |
| Take notes on all that occurs. | Takes notes and ask questions. Note errors that occur so they can be corrected. |
| Use and elicit "we" behaviors. | Demonstrate "we" attitude. |
| Exercise follow-up options if consensus can't be reached on an issue. | Suggest closure for items that aren't resolved within allotted time; volunteer for follow-up tasks that are assigned. |

# 4

## The Meeting Process: The RE–7 Approach

So far in this book we have introduced you to some of the basic concepts about meetings and about the people who lead them and attend them. In this chapter, we will discuss the meeting process itself, the *measures* or *steps* that must be taken to ensure a successful outcome.

These measures can be summarized in the "RE–7" approach to meetings, a seven-step approach that will facilitate your meeting planning and help you measure the effectiveness of your meetings. Note that each of the critical steps in this approach begins with the letters "re." This mnemonic device will help you to better remember each measure.

1. Required?
2. Readiness
3. Restraints
4. Record
5. Regulate
6. Review
7. Results

The first step, asking yourself whether a meeting is really required, is the most crucial step in the approach. If you can think of an alternative to holding the meeting, then the meeting process can quickly come to a halt and valuable time and money can be saved. On the other hand, if you determine that a meeting is the most expedient way to handle the items in question, you can work through the remaining six measures to ensure that your meeting flows smoothly and produces successful results (Fig. 8). Each of the seven measures is discussed in detail in this chapter.

*"Too many meetings are held each month for no better reason than it is has been a month since the last one."*

**—Anonymous**

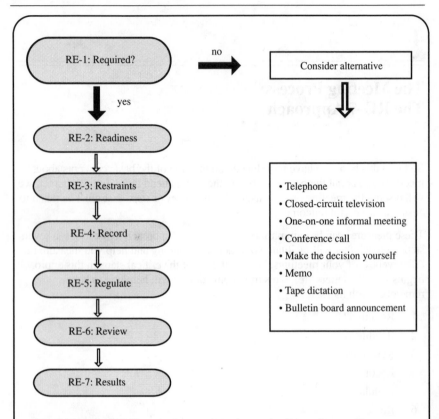

**Fig. 8**. Using the "RE-7" approach to meetings, the meeting planner first considers whether a meeting is really required. Such an approach can help to eliminate many costly, unnecessary meetings.

## RE–1: Required?

As we have emphasized, the meeting planner must begin—always—by measuring or evaluating the *need* for a meeting. It is foolhardy and wasteful to call meetings when information can be disseminated, shared, or created in some other way. All too often, we meet merely because it has been a week or a month since the last meeting. Ask yourself the following questions to evaluate whether a meeting is really necessary:

- What projects are people working on now?
- Is an hour spent on those projects more valuable than an hour spent in a meeting?

- If given a choice between meeting and working on their projects, what would the staff members select?
- Are we planning this meeting simply because it is always held at this time, or is there a valid reason for calling this meeting?
- What were the results of the last meeting we held?
- How much time do staff members spend in meetings each week?
- What is the cost to the organization of having this meeting?
- Will the meeting's output justify this cost?

If you decide that a meeting really is not necessary, consider using one of the following alternatives to deliver your message:

- Telephone
- Closed-circuit television
- One-on-one informal meeting
- Conference call
- Making the decision yourself
- Memo
- Tape dictation
- Bulletin board announcement

The last option, a bulletin board announcement, is being used quite successfully in a number of workplaces. You can color-code a bulletin board and divide it into three sections. The first section, which may be red, for example, could contain vital information; it is the responsibility of the employees to check that section daily to ensure they are apprised of important changes, policies, and other matters. Should an employee feel further clarification of an announcement is needed, he or she is responsible for bringing questions to the supervisor.

The middle section, coded in another color, could contain information that is not urgent but must be read nonetheless. Employees need not check that section daily but are still responsible for the notices posted there.

The final section, which could be coded in yet another color, would be for employee use. Here, employees could post information about retirement parties, articles for sale, ride-sharing needs, and so forth.

This bulletin board system reduces considerably the need for information-giving meetings.

## RE–2: Readiness

Once it has been decided that a meeting is required, it must be organized and planned. *Efficient* meetings are the result of careful planning. The meeting planner must attend to a number of details to ensure "readiness," including:

- Defining the meeting's purpose.

- Selecting participants.
- Appointing monitors.
- Choosing a time and place.
- Preparing an agenda.
- Rehearsing.
- Attending to physical arrangements.
- Sending out notices.

We will discuss these details point by point in the next few pages.

### Defining the Meeting's Purpose

To prepare for the convening of others around a common goal, the planner starts with the purpose. He or she must be clear about the meeting's objective, the expected outcome, or the problem to be solved.

Remind yourself and others of the saying that Ronald Reagan kept in the Oval Office: "It's amazing how much you can accomplish if you do not care who gets the credit." This observation may encourage participants to put aside their egos and personal motives and band together to accomplish the business of the company.

When contemplating the purpose, think, too, about which type of meeting can best accommodate the purpose (information-giving, information-sharing, information-creating). Decide in advance which leadership approach (autocratic, democratic, laissez-faire) and which communication style (bull's-eye, ping-pong, spiral) can contribute to the meeting's success. Don't neglect to think about which individuals can assume the leadership of the meeting at various points.

In addition to defining the purpose, the conscientious meeting planner knows beforehand which measures can be used to evaluate whether that purpose was met, or in other words, whether the meeting was successful. If, for example, you call a meeting so the staff can prepare a position paper on a specific issue and by the end of the meeting that paper has been written, you can deem your meeting a success. Generally speaking, if you did what you set out to do, the meeting accomplished its purpose. But you cannot measure the accomplishment until you have clearly specified the purpose. The Meeting Evaluation Form in Appendix B can be distributed to meeting participants. The feedback it provides will help you measure the productivity of your meetings.

### Selecting Participants

Having clearly established the meeting's purpose, the planner thinks next about who should be invited. Invite only those who can profit from the meeting either because they can make a contribution or because they can learn from what will transpire. This is not the time to worry about hurting the feelings of those you do not invite.

Meetings are opportunities for new managers to observe firsthand how company business is conducted and to see how they themselves will be expected to interact and present ideas.

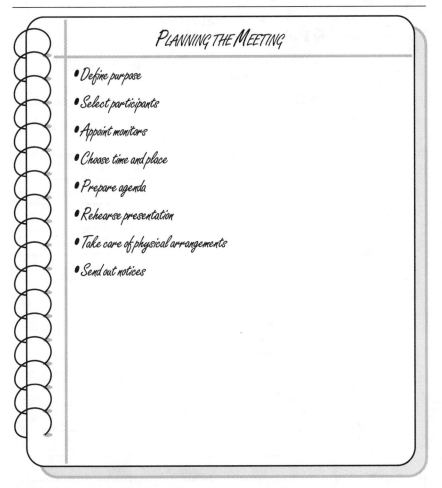

*Planning the Meeting*

- Define purpose
- Select participants
- Appoint monitors
- Choose time and place
- Prepare agenda
- Rehearse presentation
- Take care of physical arrangements
- Send out notices

The astute planner will anticipate the behaviors of those who will be involved in the meeting. If you expect, for example, that two people are likely to get into a dispute, meet with them beforehand to iron out differences so that valuable meeting time will not be wasted. Anticipate the objections certain members are likely to make about particular items and be ready to address those objections.

Keep in mind our earlier discussions about the number and kinds of people who should attend the meeting, depending on its purpose (see the summary grid at the end of Chapter 2). If, for example, the meeting is essentially an information-giving one, surely a larger number of participants can be accommodated since pertinent information about the company's mission needs to be disseminated. Invite a smaller number, however, if a specific issue needs to be discussed or if the meeting will be a working meeting.

If you have invited individuals who are unfamiliar with the meeting's topic, brief them *before* the meeting begins so that time will not be wasted bringing them up to date.

## ✍ Worksheet 9
## Meeting Participation: Making A Contribution

It has been said that if you can't contribute to a meeting, you should exit.
How do you feel about this? Record your thoughts here.

_____

_____

_____

_____

_____

_____

_____

_____

_____

_____

_____

_____

_____

_____

_____

_____

_____

_____

_____

_____

_____

_____

_____

## Appointing Monitors

As long as human beings attend meetings, there will be the temptation to disregard agenda topics and times and get caught up in a particular point of contention or special interest. For this reason, we urge you to review the list of those who will be attending and select one person as the *time monitor* and another as the *topic monitor*. These two individuals will be responsible for ensuring that everyone adheres to the topics on the agenda within the recommended time frames.

> *"The length of a meeting rises with the square of the number of people present."*
>
> **— Anonymous**

In general, the time monitor should:

- Have an agenda with time allocations indicated for each item open for discussion.
- Be assertive enough to keep others on target.
- Not have a vested interest in the topic.
- Bring a watch.

Likewise, the topic monitor should:

- Meet in advance with the meeting leader to ensure understanding of the meeting's purpose and goals.
- Be able to identify nonproductive discussions.
- Have a firm, but inoffensive manner.
- Be able to periodically restate the progress that has been made.

If issues arise that are important but not scheduled, they may be tabled until the next meeting. Such topics could also be investigated by an ad hoc group (appointed when the topics arise) that reports back to the larger group at the next meeting.

## Choosing a Time and Place

It is nearly impossible to find a time and place that suits everyone, but there are some steps that you, as the meeting planner, can take to help reduce disgruntlement.

Before setting a time, you may wish to poll those invited and then choose a time that seems to be convenient for the most people. To avoid carping, forewarn everyone that the majority vote will rule.

If the meeting is scheduled to be long, divide it up, ideally with a major break such as lunch. It may even be better to hold such a meeting on two separate days.

As a rule of thumb, avoid Friday afternoons and prelunch meetings, as attendees will be anxious to end the meeting on time and may not give their full attention to the matters under discussion. Postlunch meetings can be difficult as well, since some people will probably be late and others may not be attuned to the matters at hand if they have eaten a heavy lunch. (Chronobiologists tell us that people experience a "postprandial letdown" right after lunch that prevents operating at peak efficiency.)

As with the meeting time, the meeting location should be one that is convenient for the most people. It should be well-ventilated, have comfortable seating, and be large enough to allow some movement among participants. Ideally, everyone should be able to sit around a conference table and have access to a writing surface.

*"The more boring the subject, the longer the meeting will run."*

**— Murphy**

Occasionally, off-site meetings, though they may cost more in terms of both time and money, are worth the investment. If your meeting or conference merits special attention, give some thought to holding it at an off-site hotel or conference center. Meeting there will certainly eliminate the distractions and interruptions that occur when meeting in the office. Also, selecting such a location suggests to the participants that the meeting is not just a run-of-the-mill assembly of the usual people for the usual reasons.

### Preparing an Agenda

A single sheet of paper, the agenda, marks the difference between the professional and the unprofessional planner of meetings, for it reflects the seriousness with which the meeting planner approaches the meeting. The agenda should be distributed at least twenty-four hours prior to the meeting.

An agenda may take many forms. Some are more detailed than others. The sample agenda in Figure 9 states the meeting's purpose, shows the various topics to be covered, who will present them, and the discussion time allotted for each. Some agendas also include any materials that attendees should bring or any advance preparation that may be necessary for a particular topic.

In addition, experienced meeting planners formulate a few questions for each item on the agenda in case the participants fail to discuss the issues in depth. Likewise, a planner who thinks ahead will build in time for nonagenda discussions that might arise. Listing the time allotment beside each item helps keep the participants focused. It also suggests that the meeting leader has prioritized the items, as reflected by the amount of time allocated to each. If possible, try to limit the meeting to an hour, as studies show that efficiency and attention tend to drop after the first sixty minutes. If the meeting happens to conclude before the scheduled time, then by all means, disband!

### Rehearsing

If you plan to make a presentation during the meeting, you must rehearse what you will say. You may do this in several ways:

- In front of a mirror in the privacy of your home
- In front of friends or family members who can be trusted to give you honest feedback
- With a tape recorder to hear how you sound to others
- With a video recorder to see how you appear to others

**Quality Partnerships Corporation**

Regular Meeting of Quality Partnerships Committee
Wednesday, March 11, at 5:30 p.m.

### AGENDA

| | | |
|---|---|---|
| 5:30 | Call to order | Leslie Bay |
| | Roll call | |
| 5:35 | Reading of minutes of February 25 meeting | |
| 5:45 | Committee or individual reports | |
| 5:45 | A. Treasurer's report | Bill Chenley |
| 5:50 | B. Report on lunchtime seminars | Connie Stampley |
| 5:55 | C. Report on meeting at Downley Chemicals | Frank Critten |
| 6:05 | Continuing business | |
| | A. Expansion of Committee membership | Connie Stampley |
| 6:15 | New business | |
| | A. Involvement of local educational institutions in Committee activities | Jim Cross |
| 6:25 | Announcements | |
| | A. Place, date, and time of next meeting | |
| 6:30 | Adjournment | |

**Fig. 9.** An agenda is essential to keeping a meeting on course. It should allot time for the call to order, roll call, reading of minutes, committee and individual reports, continuing business, new business, and announcements.

## Attending to Physical Arrangements

Successful meetings are not the result of happenstance; they are the result of careful preparation and planning. Physical arrangements must be considered along with the agenda. The meeting planner will have to make decisions about these key items:

- Room reservation
- Size of the room
- Air-conditioning/heating
- Materials the participants may need (paper, pens, name cards, water, coffee, refreshments)
- Audiovisual equipment and its placement
- Extra bulbs for the projector, a full pad of paper on the flip chart, pointers, marking pens, chalk, and eraser
- Acoustics
- Lighting
- "No smoking" signs, ashtrays, or a separate smoking section
- Information regarding directions, parking, location of phones, restaurants, restrooms, etc.
- Signs or notices to be posted in the building in which the meeting will be held to help attendees find the meeting room
- Shape of the table(s)
- Kinds and number of chairs
- Arrangement of the chairs/tables if the meeting is a large one

There are numerous ways to arrange the seating. Before making a final decision about the arrangement of the chairs and/or tables, ask yourself these simple questions:

- What is the purpose of the meeting?
- What chairs and tables are available?
- How many people will be attending?
- How has the seating arrangement been handled in the past?
- What is the leader's or speaker's preference?
- What physical constraints will limit the arrangement?
- Will the attendees need to work in small groups?
- Will a "breakout" room be needed?
- Will the leader or speaker move around the room?
- Will attendees need to move around the room?

A few possible room arrangements are presented in Figure 10. The larger the group, the more likely the seating will be auditorium-style rows of chairs. If the group is expected to take notes or create information, chairs arranged around a table would clearly be a better choice.

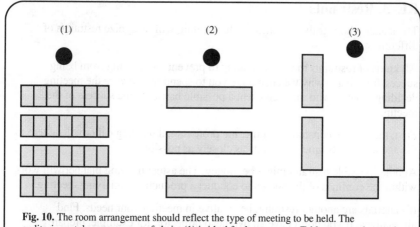

**Fig. 10.** The room arrangement should reflect the type of meeting to be held. The auditorium-style arrangement of chairs (1) is ideal for large groups. Tables arranged around the lecturer's podium (2 and 3) are more suited for smaller groups that will be required to take notes and participate in discussions.

## Sending Out Notices

The notice, or announcement, of the meeting, can take the form of an informal agenda. The notice can also require each person who is invited to do something to prepare for the meeting. For example, at the bottom of the agenda announcement, one of these requests may be noted:

- Please come prepared with a one- to two-minute statement reflecting your views on this topic.

- I will expect each of you to provide three original solutions that might be implemented to solve the problem.

- Our choices on these issues are limited. Please have ready a statement of projected consequences for each of the choices available to us.

- This event/issue/ruling has a potentially serious impact on our organization. Please prepare a list of three ways we can offset the possible negative outcomes.

Of course, those who are invited should also be asked to bring any documents that are relevant to the topics being discussed. And, if various members will be called on to make a contribution at certain points, their names should be written on the agenda along with the time allotted for their presentations.

You may wish to send out a premeeting survey to help you in the planning process (see Appendix B). If colleagues are permitted to return the survey without identifying themselves, you may be able to obtain some honest reactions and valuable insights into the meeting process in your organization. The survey included in the Appendix may be copied and distributed or used as a basis for designing your own premeeting survey.

## RE–3: Restraints

The leader who is truly in control of the meeting will recognize restraints of different sorts.

All kinds of restraints may be operating to prevent the meeting from being successful. That is why we encourage you to spend time *before* the meeting deciding what or who may represent a possible barrier to the success of the meeting.

First, there is the constraint of time: the professional meeting caller will adhere to the agenda and its time allotments as closely as possible.

Another possible restraint might be money. The astute meeting planner will work within the confines of the budget to conduct a productive, satisfying meeting.

If materials are another restraint, be creative in meeting your needs. Find alternatives. If you don't have an overhead projector, for example, prepare diagrams on chart paper. If you don't have a slide projector, see if you can borrow or rent one.

If you are restrained by the size of the room, consider postponing the meeting until the room you need is available. Or meet in the private dining area of a nearby restaurant. Even consider using your own home and combining the meeting with a social event.

Perhaps the most important restraint, in terms of its impact on a meeting's outcome, is self-restraint—on the part of both the leader and the participants. The following chart (Fig. 11) depicts the leader's responsibilities and the various roles he or she plays in restraining the group and keeping its energy directed toward the meeting's goals. As the chart shows, the leader should be equally a supporter, catalyst, stimulator, harmonizer, and facilitator.

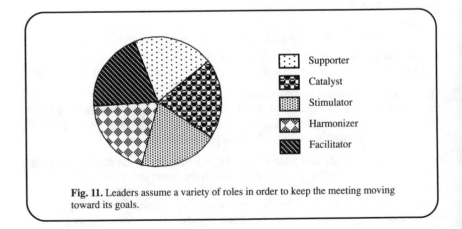

**Fig. 11.** Leaders assume a variety of roles in order to keep the meeting moving toward its goals.

At this point, you may wish to review Chapter 3, which deals with some of the positive behaviors meeting leaders and participants can display. Chapter 3 also offers suggestions for dealing with situations and character types that have the potential to damage a meeting's outcome.

## RE–4: Record

Ideas are generated so quickly during the course of meetings that unless someone is appointed to record what is transpiring, valuable ideas are bound to be lost. That goes without saying. People cannot be trusted to remember everything that occurs during an hour-long meeting in which numerous contributions are made by numerous individuals. Events are often recorded by an organization's elected secretary, but another individual may be appointed as the minute-taker instead.

Because the minutes become the official record of the meeting, it is important that the minute-taker record events with precision and accuracy. Once the minutes have been approved, they can be used as a basis for confirming votes and for establishing precedents, among other things.

The minute-taker, however, need not become weighed down by every detail if he or she can focus on these questions (Fig. 12):

- Who attended?
- What decisions were agreed on?
- What assignments were made and to whom?
- What will be the topic for the next meeting?
- When will the next meeting be held?
- Who will be attending?

The minutes should be distributed within twenty-four hours of the meeting.

Each meeting also needs a scribe, a person who writes on chart paper the various discussion points that will eventually lead to a decision and/or a course of action. The appointment of a scribe is especially important for information-creating meetings. The scribe—and other appointees such as a timekeeper—should be individuals with no vested interest in the meeting's action.

While the minute-taker records the official results of the more formalized discussion points, the scribe helps others to focus on what the discussion points should be. Without the scribe's efforts, there might not *be* any results to put into the minutes. It is the scribe who propels the meeting's action forward, by listing ideas that will later be molded into manageable focal points or categories.

In a brainstorming session, for example, someone needs to record group member's thoughts before they are lost. It is the scribe who assists in this idea-gathering stage by listing the ideas on a flip chart as fast as he or she possibly can. Afterwards, when the group has agreed on the two or three ideas that will be pursued further, those two or three ideas become part of the official minutes. The minute-taker is essentially concerned with the refined products of the scribe's idea-listing process.

## Quality Partnerships Corporation

The meeting of the Quality Partnerships Committee was called to order by the Chair, Leslie Bay, at 5:30 p.m. on Wednesday, March 11. In attendance were Thomas Quay, Frank Critten, Susan Edd, Barbara Erte, Jim Cross, Bill Chenley, Theresa Kilian, and Connie Stampley. The minutes of the last meeting were read and accepted.

The Treasurer's report was read and accepted as amended. We currently have $1,845.32 in the operating budget for the year and $2,356.98 that has been raised for the scholarship fund. Funds from the sale of T-shirts will be used to send one committee member to a Quality workshop.

Connie Stampley reported that her proposal to have lunchtime seminars is being reviewed by upper management. If approval is given, letters will be sent to area colleges inviting speakers to address small groups of employees on various Quality issues. The following topics were suggested for the lunchtime lecture series: *The Common Language of Quality, Dealing with Suppliers, Universal Participation,* and *Satisfying the Internal Customer.*

Frank Critten reported on the meeting he had attended at Downley Chemicals. Representatives from five other corporations were present. The group's goal is the formation of a Quality symposium, which would sponsor an annual Quality consortium. The Committee voted to allocate $500 to help with start-up costs. The other corporations were expected to make equal contributions.

Connie Stampley proposed that a vote be taken on the tabled question of the size of the Quality Partnerships Committee. She moved that membership be expanded to twelve individuals from any level of the organization. Barbara Erte seconded the motion, which passed unanimously.

The final agenda topic was the involvement of local educational institutions in the activities of the Quality Partnerships Committee. A motion was made by Jim Cross, and seconded by Susan Edd, to invite an area high school teacher to attend committee meetings. Thomas Quay volunteered to contact area principals regarding educators who may be interested in joining the Committee.

The next meeting will be held on Wednesday, March 25.

Respectfully submitted,

Theresa Kilian, Secretary

**Fig. 12.** The minutes are the official record of the events that transpire during a meeting.

# RE–5: Regulate

As the meeting leader, you will be expected to regulate the flow of events. You are responsible for seeing that the meeting moves along toward its goals by the appointed time. Other participants expect you to keep the meeting from floundering, whether it be through dissension or pointless discussion. We recommend these twenty-two strategies for keeping your meetings on target and on time.

## Meeting Strategies

1. Appoint a facilitator or topic monitor to remind the group when it is straying from the topic at hand. This person should be neutral as far as the issues are concerned.

2. Appoint a time monitor to caution the group when the time allocations are being exceeded. Like the topic monitor, this person should not be overly involved with the issues so that he or she can concentrate on keeping track of time.

3. Start the meeting on time.

4. Don't waste time politely reviewing what has already been covered for those who arrive late.

5. Stick to the agenda and its time frame. Table nonagenda items until the next meeting.

6. Minimize distractions, both real and potential.

7. Be sensitive to the group's need to take a break or to end the meeting. Group members will indicate such needs by being easily distracted, restless, or argumentative. When participants begin to gather their materials, look openly (not furtively) at their watches, and have a glazed look in their eyes, you should begin to wrap up the proceedings.

8. Do what you can to maintain the group's interest.

9. Discuss the unimportant items on the agenda quickly.

10. Do not permit one individual to dominate the meeting.

11. Watch out for "group think"; don't allow group conformity to control decision making.

12. Be sure appropriate problem-solving procedures are being used. After evidence of a problem has been presented, interpret it and then decide which actions should be followed.

13. Attack problems, not the people who cause them.

14. Be aware of extremes: groups that are too divided, too united, or too task-oriented do not function as well as groups that are moderated.

15. Avoid these communication barriers:

    • Words that may have multiple interpretations

    • Generalizations (words such as "always" or "never")

    • Sexist language

    • Presenting information without first providing a framework for it

16. Be firm with ramblers.

17. Ignore irrelevant comments.

18. Continually summarize points that have been made or agreements that have been reached.

19. If you feel you are being put on the spot, give the question right back to the person who asked it. For example, you might ask, "How would you handle it?"

20. If the group is growing restless or if interest in the topic is waning, ask open-ended questions.

21. Reinforce or repeat points of discussion that parallel the meeting's purpose.

22. If two participants disagree to the point of conflict, try one of these tactics:

    • Call for a vote on the matter.

    • Introduce a diversion, such as taking a break.

    • Try humor.

    • Have the parties who disagree leave the room to carry on their discussion.

    • Ask for facts rather than emotion-based opinions.

    • Clarify the areas of disagreement.

    • Insist that one person talk without being interrupted. Then allow the other person the same courtesy.

## ✍ Worksheet 10
## Regulating Problems During Meetings

Are you causing any of these meeting problems? If so, jot down ways to solve them. If someone else is the source of the problem, note what you might do to improve the situation.

- Too much interrupting
- Did not start on time
- Did not end on time
- No follow up
- Meeting not appropriate for my needs
- No serious listening
- No summary
- Vague assignments ("Someone look into this next week.")
- Leader unprepared

- People came in late
- No breaks
- No coffee
- No time or willingness to deal with unanticipated issues
- Leader scolded or argued with attendees
- Scheduled at a terrible time
- Sarcastic comments stifled creativity
- "Group think" prevented real consideration of issues

_____

_____

_____

_____

_____

_____

_____

_____

_____

_____

_____

_____

_____

## RE–6: Review

How do you, as the meeting planner, prevent ideas or assignments from slipping through the cracks? By *reviewing* what has been accomplished and agreed on. This review should take place at several points during the meeting and again before the meeting is adjourned. The leader should also periodically check to ensure that all participants understand the points that have been discussed. From time to time, ask whether anyone has questions.

Before the meeting is adjourned, review what has been discussed—possibly even using visuals—to establish that everyone agrees on the actions to be taken (Fig. 13). By forming such consensus, you pave the way for a successful next meeting, the time and place for which you should establish at this point, if possible.

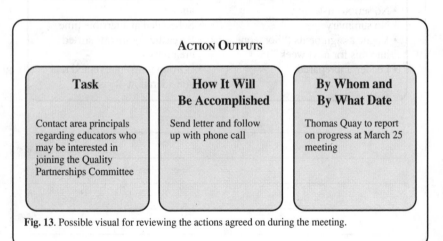

**Fig. 13**. Possible visual for reviewing the actions agreed on during the meeting.

The Meeting Evaluation Form is one more way to gauge the effectiveness of the meeting. The leader who is truly interested in obtaining feedback to ameliorate his or her meeting style will distribute an evaluation form such as the one printed in Appendix B. The form allows participants to review what transpired during the meeting. It also allows the leader to compare his or her intentions for the meeting with what the participants believe was accomplished.

Once the meeting process has been fine-tuned and the leader feels he or she is truly capable of conducting meetings that are productive, the evaluation form no longer needs to be distributed.

## RE–7: Results

As far as a successful meeting is concerned, it's not over when it's over. It's over only after the leader has carried out certain postmeeting responsibilities. Just as an award-winning film is a melding of three equally important phases— preproduction, production, and postproduction—so is a praiseworthy meeting a combination of planning, execution, and follow up. In this last stage, the meeting leader attends to several tasks during the week following the meeting.

First, review the minutes and distribute them to all attendees within twenty-four hours. Also distribute to others who may be interested, including superiors, who should be kept informed. Individuals who were invited to the meeting but were unable to attend should also receive a copy of the minutes.

As we discussed previously, the minutes become a record of the proceedings of a particular gathering of individuals. Correctly written, they provide unanimity of thought on those proceedings, thereby eliminating confusion or the temptation for some people to say that they were not given an assignment or that they don't remember the specific items that were discussed.

Next, ask a meeting participant—someone you can trust to be honest—to share with you his or her observations of the meeting's flow, its strong and weak points, and your own role as meeting leader. This individual should tell you what was accomplished—or not accomplished—and why. If the meeting met your stated goal, your "adviser" should be able to explain how the results of the meeting fit into the corporate mission.

Finally, phone individuals who volunteered for or were assigned specific tasks to see whether they have begun work on their assignments. If they have made enough strides that a progress report is warranted, consider distributing the report to those with a "need to know."

## Summary

The following grid highlights the steps in the "RE–7" approach to meetings and outlines the actions the meeting leader must take as he or she plans and organizes the meeting. Remember, conscientiously addressing each of the steps will help to ensure the meeting's successful outcome.

| "RE-7" APPROACH TO MEETINGS | |
|---|---|
| **Measure** | **Actions to Be Taken** |
| RE-1:<br>Required? | • Decide whether the meeting is necessary.<br>• If meeting is not necessary, consider alternative. |
| RE-2:<br>Readiness | • Define the purpose.<br>• Select participants.<br>• Appoint monitors.<br>• Choose a time and place.<br>• Prepare an agenda.<br>• Rehearse.<br>• Attend to physical arrangements.<br>• Send out notices. |
| RE-3:<br>Restraints | • Before the meeting begins, consider and find solutions to restraints that might prevent a successful outcome:<br>–Time<br>–Money<br>–Materials<br>–Room size<br>–Self-restraint |
| RE-4:<br>Record | • Appoint a person to take the minutes.<br>• Appoint a scribe to record discussion points leading to a course of action. |
| RE-5:<br>Regulate | • Control the flow of events so the meeting achieves goals within the allotted time. |
| RE-6:<br>Review | • During the meeting, periodically review the main discussion points and the decisions that have been made.<br>• At the end of the meeting, summarize again the major points and distribute the Meeting Evaluation Form to collect feedback about the meeting's effectiveness.<br>• After the meeting, study the feedback you obtain. |
| RE-7:<br>Results | • Distribute minutes within 24 hours.<br>• Ask a meeting participant to share with you his or her opinion of the meeting's effectiveness, its strong and weak points.<br>• Check by phone the progress of individuals who were assigned tasks. |

# 5

## Putting It All Together: Making Your Meetings Work

We began this book by asking you to consider the best and the worst meetings you have attended and to assess the factors that led you to those considerations. We also asked you to consider some common complaints about meetings and to think about what you can do to lessen the possibility of complaints at the next meeting you attend or convene.

Then, in Chapter 2, we addressed some of the basic concepts underlying meetings, including some common misconceptions and complaints that add to a meeting's cost. In Chapter 3, we examined some leader and participant behaviors that contribute to successful meetings. Finally, in Chapter 4, we discussed the steps in the "RE–7" approach to meetings.

To provoke your thinking as you worked through each chapter, we interspersed a number of quotes expressing various opinions about meetings and those who attend them. Some quotes were clearly intended tongue-in-cheek. Others, however, should have forced you to examine your organization's meeting processes and to decide whether your organization is maximizing its potential for high-powered meeting results.

### Drawing Your Own Conclusions

By this time, then, you have no doubt clarified some of your thoughts about meetings—about their value and cost, about the responsibilities of the people who lead and attend them, and about the steps in the meeting process itself. In this final chapter, designed primarily as a "working" chapter, you will be given an opportunity to "put together" the concepts we have analyzed throughout the book.

*"A meeting is really a peer-level review. It's very revealing. You can see how someone thinks, how he answers a difficult question, and whether he is an ordinary thinker."*

— Frank Considine

The worksheets in this chapter are designed to help you further clarify your thoughts and to develop concrete ideas for improving future meetings—if you have not already begun to do so.

To begin, we offer several ideas for raising meeting awareness in your organization. Worksheet 11 asks you to consider some of those ideas and to formulate specific steps for implementing them into your organization's meeting process. Worksheet 12 asks you to consider how your opinions about meetings have changed as a result of reading this book and allows you to draw your own conclusions about the measures you can take to create successful meetings. Finally, Worksheet 13 asks you to read the script of a fictional meeting and to use what you have learned to critique or evaluate the meeting. A sample critique is included at the end of the exercise.

As you work through this final chapter, applying the concepts in this book to real meeting situations, remember this: It only takes one person to start a march and—no matter what your position in your organization—you *can* make a difference. You *can* have an impact on the way things are done. Successful results can be achieved, but not without a great deal of practice and rehearsal to eliminate the minor irritants.

You *can* cause others to marvel at the synergistic power that is released when you bring people together. But you must first think through the hazards and pitfalls and then undertake the measures that will ultimately yield *meetings that work.*

## Ideas for Raising Meeting Awareness

If, by this time, you feel you have pinpointed the weak areas of your meetings but are still groping for specific or creative ways to improve them, consider some of the ideas presented in this section.

The innovative ideas presented here should be considered carefully. While each of these suggestions for raising meeting awareness is being used somewhere in an American corporation, we issue this caveat: only you know the culture of your corporation and the nature of the individuals who operate within that culture. Although these ideas are more creative than revolutionary—designed to bring a bit of vitality to meetings that have lacked excitement in the past—each could also backfire if not used under the proper circumstances with the proper meeting participants.

On the other hand, the suggestions can bring dramatic results to your next meeting; they will ensure that people will long remember your efforts to make meetings interesting and worthwhile. We don't expect you to try every one of these twenty-nine ideas for bringing zest to the conference room, but we do hope you will commit to trying *some* of them. The difference between "fizzle" and "sizzle" can be *you*.

1. Lock out latecomers. The word will quickly spread that you expect to start meetings on time.

2. Set a timer and conclude the meeting when it rings.

3. Show a training video about meetings or any other pertinent topic.

4. Have a guest speaker.

5. Bring in an outsider (customer, salesperson, vendor, another department representative) who can bring an unusual perspective to the issues being discussed.

6. Calculate how much the meeting is costing the company (be sure to add in the cost of fringe benefits) and announce that figure before the meeting begins.

7. Deliberately set up a person in the back of the room who will confront or contradict the most important points you are making. (This technique is especially galvanizing with speakers who are not known for their histrionic abilities.) The rapid-fire exchange between you and that challenger will surely enliven a soporific topic.

8. On the memo sent out to announce the meeting, write the following statement: "Please attend this meeting only if you feel you can make a contribution or if you feel you can profit from attending." Then sit back and wait to see who shows up.

9. Knowing that some restaurants deliberately have hard seats so customers will not linger, thereby preventing other customers from being seated, try using uncomfortable chairs so the meeting can be conducted with little wasted time.

10. Go one step further and have a meeting with no chairs!

11. Put an hourglass on the table and adjourn the meeting when all the sand has trickled to the bottom.

12. Permit no interruptions or questions until the end of the meeting.

13. Invite your boss to sit in as an observer.

14. Turn the air conditioning off (or down to 60°).

15. Hold the meeting on a Saturday.

16. Stop at the halfway point and ask each person, "How is this meeting working for you so far?"

17. If the meeting is information-giving in nature, have a leaderless meeting. Tape-record the information and leave the tape and a recorder in the middle of the conference room table.

18. Use a round table if you are not already doing so.

19. Require each participant to publicly pledge what he or she will do for the next meeting.

20. Obtain a starter's pistol (used at track races) and fire it each time there is a lag in the meeting.

21. Schedule the meeting one hour before lunch or before quitting time on Friday and ensure the meeting concludes on time.

22. Have participants fill out evaluation forms. Study the responses so you can make serious improvements in the next meeting.

23. If the meeting is an information-creating one, make certain you have the ideal mix of high-IQ, highly-creative, highly-practical attendees.

24. Order in delicate pastries or a special lunch or roses.

25. Ask each participant to come to the meeting prepared with a statement of his or her opinion on the issues or problems on the agenda.

26. Stagger the attendance of individuals who may have reports to make. Those people then will not have to waste time attending meetings for matters that do not pertain to them, and the other meeting members will be forced to adhere to the scheduled times.

27. Use name cards and force attendees to sit in places other than their usual ones.

28. If you always have scheduled staff meetings on Friday mornings or the first Monday of every month, skip one such meeting and ask the usual participants to submit a brief activity report instead.

29. At each meeting, have a different attendee fill out the Meeting Evaluation Form and meet with you privately to discuss its contents.

*"Thou shalt not meet for more than one hour."*

**—The Eleventh Commandment**

# ✍ Worksheet 11
## Implementing Innovative Ideas

Which of the ideas discussed in this chapter would you try to implement in
your organization? What steps would you need to follow to achieve
successful implementation? Use the space below to record your thoughts.

_____

_____

_____

_____

_____

_____

_____

_____

_____

_____

_____

_____

_____

_____

_____

_____

_____

_____

_____

_____

_____

_____

_____

## ✍ Worksheet 12
## Making Your Meetings Work

Did you find your opinions about meetings changing as you worked through the various exercises in this book? Now that you have read the book completely, use this exercise to sort through the information we have presented and to draw your own conclusions about it. Then decide which measures to implement in *your* organization's meeting process and the results you want those measures to produce.

1.  These are ways in which my opinions about meetings have changed:

    _____

    _____

    _____

    _____

    _____

2.  These are the measures I will undertake before, during, and after my next meeting:

    _____

    _____

    _____

    _____

    _____

3.  These are the results I hope those measures will help to achieve in my next meeting:

    _____

    _____

    _____

    _____

    _____

## ✍ Worksheet 13
## Meeting Script Critique

As you read the following dialogue, use the right-hand column to make notes about the meeting's effectiveness. Let your comments reflect some of the information you have acquired from *Meetings That Work*. At the end of the dialogue, you will be asked to provide a general critique of the meeting.

**NOTES**

*John:* I'm glad each of you could attend this meeting. Ordinarily, I would not expect you to show up with no advance notice, but a special situation has arisen and I need to have your input. There is no real agenda here so feel free to jump in with your ideas at any time.

*Tom:* Can I ask why we are here? It *is* 5:30 and most of us were just about ready to head home.

*John:* I was just getting to that. We've had a tragedy occur in our Plainview office and in view of that, it is imperative for us to formulate—as quickly as possible—some plans for dealing with a similar eventuality.

*Camille:* Don't keep us in suspense, John. Tell us what happened.

*John:* Let me preface my remarks by assuring each and every one of you that what I am about to describe is not an isolated occurrence. It could happen here as easily as it happened in Plainview. But rest assured that I, and the other members of the senior management team, are doing everything within our power to . . .

*Ann (interrupting):* John, could you please get to the point. I can feel a migraine coming on and I'd like to get some aspirin.

*Belinda (whispering):* Ann, I didn't know you suffered from migraines. So do I. Do you eat a lot of cheese? My doctor, Dr. Swertle, told me that cheese and chocolate and caffeine are the primary causes of migraines.

*John (loudly):* As I was saying, we are doing everything within our power to ensure that a similar incident does not occur in our facility.

*Kim:* And, just what *was* that incident, John?

*John:* Well . . . (pausing dramatically), Bob Bwerk has been stabbed.

*Sue:* STABBED? You mean, KILLED?

*John:* Well, no. Thank goodness, he was not killed.

*Kim:* Just how serious are his injuries?

*John:* Well . . . he has two puncture wounds!

*Sue:* Omigawd! Where? Not in the heart, I hope!

*John:* Actually, the wounds did not affect his vital areas, but they could have.

*Kim:* Exactly where was he wounded, John, and how did it happen?

*John:* Well…he was stabbed in the buttocks.

*Kim:* And can you tell us what prompted the "end" result?

*John:* No, I can't reveal that information yet, but it has something to do with a firing.

*Ann:* John, do you think we could discuss this first thing tomorrow morning? I agree that it is important, but I have to pick up my son from the nursery. I didn't have enough time to make other arrangements.

*John:* Sure, Ann. That's no problem. You go ahead. The rest of us will just toss around some ideas for a while. We can't discuss this tomorrow because we are having an on-site inspection then, remember? And I really feel this situation merits our fullest and most immediate attention now.

*Shirley:* John, could I suggest that we divide the problem into sections and each of us take one section, think about it tonight and submit tomorrow some written recommendations for your review. Then we could meet the day after tomorrow to formulate an official plan.

*Mark:* I'd be willing to call the university's Crisis Center to see if someone could come to speak with us on Thursday about the best ways to handle people who get emotional when they hear bad news. And maybe we could get someone to talk to us about security in the office.

*Kevin:* I think all this hyperkinetic activity is just going to make people very nervous about something that will probably never happen. Just let it be. Why get everyone all upset worrying about something that would never happen here?

*Carol:* Kevin may have a point. I remember when I was on a cruise ship to the Cayman Islands. Or was it when we went on our fourth honeymoon to Alaska? No, it couldn't have been the Alaska trip because that was when we met the Weldons and they weren't there when the stabbing occurred on the Islands.

*Rick (interrupting):* Stabbings are bound to occur if you allow people to bring weapons to the office. When I was in Vietnam, we were told to carry weapons no matter where we went—even if we were only around children. You never know when someone can stab you in the back. It's a jungle out there.

*Phyllis:* Speaking of a jungle, Rick, it's a jungle out there on the freeway with the rush-hour traffic. John, you can call me at home tonight and tell me what you want me to do. I'll have it ready, but I simply cannot wait here any longer. *(She walks out the door. The others follow one by one, talking loudly to avoid hearing John's protestations.)*

If you had been John, how would you have handled this meeting? Record your thoughts in the space below.

_____

_____

_____

_____

_____

_____

## Meeting Script Critique

Compare the following critique to your thoughts about how *you* would have conducted the preceeding meeting.

John began the meeting well by thanking his coworkers for being present despite such short notice. He should have had some agenda, however, even if it were a simple, informal one. The attendees deserve to know the purpose behind his calling them together.

He was correct in deciding that a policy for dealing with a similar "tragedy" is necessary. However, since the Plainview stabbing was hardly a tragedy, the meeting to formulate a policy could have been held at a time more convenient to the employees. They probably were not in the most receptive of moods so late in the day and were undoubtedly anxious to be on the road.

It almost seems that John is enjoying his opportunity to heighten the suspense about the stabbing and so is prolonging the delivery of the news. Such an action is bound to irritate his colleagues. It seems, too, that he is deliberately misleading the group by being vague about the phrase "has been stabbed."

John should have realized that once he gave Ann permission to leave, the others would soon follow suit.

John himself should have had a plan similar to Shirley's suggestion that the problem be broken down into sections. If John had had such a plan, the meeting could have been expedited and much more would have been accomplished.

The digression about Alaska and Vietnam should not have been permitted to occur. And, finally, John's loss of control is further evinced by the mass exodus.

*"Meetings are indispensible when you don't want to do anything."*

**— J.K. Galbraith**

# Appendix A

## Meeting Preparation Checklists

Use these checklists as ready references to prepare for meetings. Copy them and keep them available in a folder or binder to use before each meeting you convene. Use the facing page of each checklist to make notes about the individual items as you attend to them (e.g., relevant phone numbers, names of individuals responsible for various tasks, list of visuals/equipment needed, etc.)

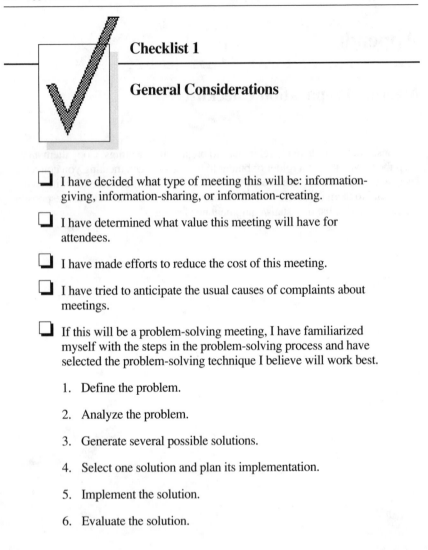

## Checklist 1

## General Considerations

☐ I have decided what type of meeting this will be: information-giving, information-sharing, or information-creating.

☐ I have determined what value this meeting will have for attendees.

☐ I have made efforts to reduce the cost of this meeting.

☐ I have tried to anticipate the usual causes of complaints about meetings.

☐ If this will be a problem-solving meeting, I have familiarized myself with the steps in the problem-solving process and have selected the problem-solving technique I believe will work best.

1. Define the problem.

2. Analyze the problem.

3. Generate several possible solutions.

4. Select one solution and plan its implementation.

5. Implement the solution.

6. Evaluate the solution.

# *NOTES*

## Checklist 2

### Is This Meeting Required?

Ask yourself the following questions to evaluate whether a meeting is really necessary:

❑ What projects are people working on now?

❑ Is an hour spent on those projects more valuable than an hour spent in a meeting?

❑ If given a choice between meeting and working on their projects, what would the staff members select?

❑ Are we planning this meeting simply because it is always held at this time, or is there a valid reason for calling this meeting?

❑ What were the results of the last meeting we held?

❑ How much time do staff members spend in meetings each week?

❑ What is the cost to the organization of having this meeting?

❑ Will the meeting's output justify this cost?

If a meeting is *not* required, which of the following would be the best alternative to a meeting?

❑ Telephone

❑ Closed-circuit television

❑ One-on-one informal meeting

❑ Conference call

❑ Making the decision myself

❑ Memo

❑ Tape dictation

❑ Bulletin board announcement

# *NOTES*

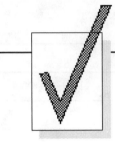

## Checklist 3

## Planning the Meeting

As the meeting leader, I have:

☐ Defined the meeting's purpose.

☐ Selected participants.

☐ Appointed monitors:

  • Time monitor
  • Topic monitor

☐ Chosen a time and place.

☐ Prepared the agenda.

☐ Rehearsed my presentation.

☐ Attended to physical arrangements:

  • Room reservation
  • Size of the room
  • Air-conditioning/heating
  • Materials the participants may need (paper, pens, name cards,
    water, coffee, refreshments)
  • Audiovisual equipment and its placement
  • Extra bulbs for the projector, a full pad of paper on the flip chart,
    pointers, marking pens, chalk, and eraser
  • Acoustics
  • Lighting
  • "No smoking" signs, ashtrays, or a separate smoking section
  • Information regarding directions, parking, location of phones,
    restaurants, restrooms, etc.
  • Signs or notices to be posted in the building in which the meeting will
    be held to help attendees find the meeting room
  • Shape of the table(s)
  • Kinds and number of chairs
  • Arrangement of the chairs/tables if the meeting is a large one

☐ Sent out notices.

# NOTES

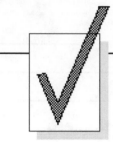

## Checklist 4

### Arranging the Meeting Room

I have considered each of the following questions pertaining to the arrangement of the tables and chairs:

❑ What is the purpose of the meeting?

❑ What chairs and tables are available?

❑ How many people will be attending?

❑ How has the seating arrangement been handled in the past?

❑ What is the leader's or speaker's preference?

❑ What physical constraints will limit the arrangement?

❑ Will the attendees need to work in small groups?

❑ Will a "breakout" room be needed?

❑ Will the leader or speaker move around the room?

❑ Will attendees need to move around the room?

# *NOTES*

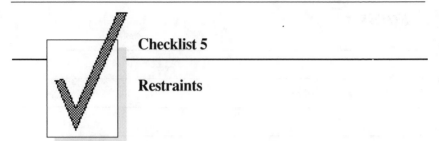

**Checklist 5**

**Restraints**

I have considered and dealt with each of the following possible barriers to a successful meeting:

 Time

❏ Money

❏ Materials

❏ Room size

❏ Self-restraint (Review Chapter 3 for suggestions on how to deal with difficult situations and various types of meeting participants as well as for leader and participant behaviors that enhance a meeting.)

# *NOTES*

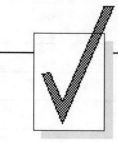

## Checklist 6

### Recording the Meeting

I have appointed a person to take minutes and have reviewed the questions he or she should focus on:

❑ Who attended?

❑ What decisions were agreed on?

❑ What assignments were made and to whom?

❑ What will be the topic for the next meeting?

❑ When will the next meeting be held?

❑ Who will be attending?

## *NOTES*

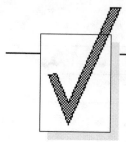

## Checklist 7

### Achieving Results

During the week following the meeting, I must:

 Distribute the minutes within twenty-four hours.

 Discuss with a trustworthy participant the strong and weak points of the meeting.

 Check the progress being made by individuals who were assigned specific tasks.

*NOTES*

# Appendix B

## Survey and Evaluation Forms

Use the forms in this section to evaluate the meetings you attend. Copy the forms and distribute them at the end of meetings. If you grant anonymity to those who complete the forms, you should obtain some honest and valuable feedback for improving your meetings. Go one step further and discuss the suggestions at your next meeting, with your supervisor, or with colleagues at other companies.

## ◆ *Premeeting Survey Form*

1. Please prioritize the items you think should be discussed at the next meeting.

_____

_____

_____

_____

_____

_____

2. Who should attend?

_____

_____

_____

3. Given the items you feel should be discussed, how much time should the meeting take? _____

4. Your preference for the meeting time: _____

   for the meeting location: _____

5. Additional comments:

_____

_____

_____

_____

_____

_____

## ◆ *Leader Evaluation Form*

1. Was an agenda distributed to participants ahead of time? —————

2. Did the meeting start on time? —————

3. Did we keep to the items and times on the agenda? —————

4. Were a time monitor and a topic monitor appointed? —————

5. Was someone appointed to take the minutes? —————

6. Was the purpose of the meeting clear? —————

7. Was there a good balance between social focus and task focus? —————

8. Were participants prepared for the meeting? —————

9. Was anyone allowed to dominate the meeting? —————

10. Was leadership shared? —————

11. Was everyone's opinion heard? —————

12. Was the meeting necessary? —————

13. Was there consensus on the items? —————

14. Did the meeting bog down at any point? If so, why? —————

—————

15. Did the leader summarize what had transpired during the meeting? —————

16. Did the meeting accomplish its purpose? —————

17. Did the participants have the right mix of intelligence, creativity, and practicality? —————

18. Did the meeting end on time? —————

Additional comments:

—————

—————

—————

—————

—————

—————

—————

◆ *Meeting Observation Form*

1. Was the meeting a success? How did the leader impact that success?

_____

_____

_____

_____

2. How well did the leader handle the various character types? What types were evident?

_____

_____

_____

3. When did the group get off the task? Why?

_____

_____

_____

_____

4. What was the climate of the meeting?

_____

_____

_____

_____

5. What improvements can you suggest?

_____

_____

_____

## ◆ *Meeting Evaluation Form*

1. What type of meeting do you think this was primarily intended to be: information-giving, information-sharing, or information-creating?

   _____

2. What do you think the meeting's specific purpose was?

   _____

3. What did you gain from this meeting?

   _____

   _____

   _____

   _____

4. Why were you invited to this meeting?

   _____

   _____

   _____

   _____

5. Do you feel the meeting accomplished its purpose?    Yes or No?

6. Were the appropriate people invited to this meeting?    Yes or No?

7. In what ways could this meeting have been improved?

   _____

   _____

   _____

   _____

8. Name (optional) _____

# Appendix C

## Meeting Agenda Planner

Agendas can take many forms. The agenda planner that follows is designed for a group or organization that meets regularly and discusses a number of items at each meeting. Agendas for meetings involving only two people or that are called to discuss one topic demanding immediate attention may not require all the features outlined here.

Bear in mind that although any agenda should be structured to keep the meeting on track and moving toward its goals, it must also be flexible. Set realistic time frames for addressing each item. Try to keep the meeting to an hour. If the meeting will be longer, schedule breaks every 90 minutes.

Do not prepare a vague agenda. Doing so only causes valuable meeting time to be used clarifying the topics and the goals to be achieved. Provide enough information about each item to allow attendees to form ideas and compile relevant data beforehand.

During the meeting, you might consider putting the agenda on a flip-chart so attendees can follow the progression of items. You can also use this flip-chart method to note solutions, decisions, and follow-up procedures.

Finally, distribute the agenda at least twenty-four hours before the meeting, but usually no more than a week before.

For your convenience, the Meeting Agenda Planner on the next six pages was designed to be photocopied.

Page 1

## *Meeting Agenda Planner*

Title of Meeting/Name of Group Meeting _____

Time (Day/Date/Time) _____

Estimated Length _____

Location (Include a map if some of those invited may be unfamiliar with the location) _____

Telephone Number Attendees Can Be Reached At During Meeting _____

Purpose of Meeting/Goals to Be Achieved _____

Attendees (List names/departments/organizations of persons invited to the meeting. Unless another format is preferred, list the names alphabetically. Be sure to note who will be leading the meeting.)

## A. Opening

| Item | Person Responsible | Time |
|------|-------------------|------|
| Call to Order | _____ | _____ |
| Welcome | _____ | _____ |
| Introductions | _____ | _____ |
| Reading/Approval of Minutes | _____ | _____ |
| Reading/Approval of Agenda | _____ | _____ |

## B. Business

## Committee Reports

| Committee | Presenter | Format (Lecture, Discussion, etc.) | Materials/ Resources | Time |
|-----------|-----------|-----------------------------------|---------------------|------|
| _____ | _____ | _____ | _____ | _____ |
| _____ | _____ | _____ | _____ | _____ |
| _____ | _____ | _____ | _____ | _____ |
| _____ | _____ | _____ | _____ | _____ |

# Individual Reports

| Item | Presenter | Format (Lecture, Discussion, etc.) | Materials/Resources | Time |
|---|---|---|---|---|
| 1. _____ | _____ | _____ | _____ | _____ |

*Description of Issue/Problem* _____

*Goal(s) to Be Accomplished* _____

| 2. _____ | _____ | _____ | _____ | _____ |

*Description of Issue/Problem* _____

*Goal(s) to Be Accomplished* _____

| 3. _____ | _____ | _____ | _____ | _____ |

*Description of Issue/Problem* _____

*Goal(s) to Be Accomplished* _____

## Continuing Business

| Item | Presenter | Format (Lecture, Discussion, etc.) | Materials/ Resources | Time |
|------|-----------|-----------------------------------|----------------------|------|
| 1. _____ | _____ | _____ | _____ | _____ |

*Description of Issue/Problem* _____

*Goal(s) to Be Accomplished* _____

| 2. _____ | | | | |

*Description of Issue/Problem* _____

*Goal(s) to Be Accomplished* _____

| 3. _____ | | | | |

*Description of Issue/Problem* _____

*Goal(s) to Be Accomplished* _____

## New Business

| Item | Presenter | Format (Lecture, Discussion, etc.) | Materials/ Resources | Time |
|------|-----------|-----------------------------------|---------------------|------|
| 1. | | | | |

*Description of Issue/Problem*

*Goal(s) to Be Accomplished*

| 2. | | | | |

*Description of Issue/Problem*

*Goal(s) to Be Accomplished*

| 3. | | | | |

*Description of Issue/Problem*

*Goal(s) to Be Accomplished*

## C. Closing

| Item | Person Responsible | Time |
|------|-------------------|------|
| Announcements | _____ | _____ |
| Place/Date/Time of Next Meeting | _____ | _____ |
| Adjournment | _____ | _____ |

**Meeting Notes**

_____

_____

_____

_____

_____

# Select from these SkillPath Books for Your Professional and Personal Growth

| Title | Item Number |
|---|---|
| **Handbooks** | |
| **A Winning Attitude:** | 12-0009 |
| *How to Develop Your Most Important Asset!* | |
| **Dynamic Delegation!** | 12-0010 |
| *A Manager's Guide For Active Empowerment* | |
| **Every Woman's Guide to Career Success** | 12-0003 |
| **Hiring and Firing:** | 12-0008 |
| *What Every Manager Needs to Know* | |
| **How to Deal With Difficult People** | 12-0004 |
| **Meetings That Work** | 12-0006 |
| **Networking:** | 12-0011 |
| *How to Creatively Tap Your People Resources* | |
| **Power Write!** | 12-0002 |
| *A Practical Guide to Words That Work* | |
| **Taking Charge:** | 12-0005 |
| *A Personal Guide to Managing Projects and Priorities* | |
| **The Supervisor's Guide** | 12-0001 |
| *The Everyday Guide to Coordinating People and Tasks* | |
| | |
| **Self-Study Sourcebooks** | |
| **Productivity Power:** | 13-0002 |
| *250 Great Ideas for Being More Productive* | |
| **Risk-Taking:** | 13-0003 |
| *50 Ways To Turn Risks Into Rewards* | |
| **Write It Right!** | 13-0001 |
| *A Guide for Clear and Correct Writing* | |

To order any of these resources, or to request a complete SkillPath BookStore catalog, call toll-free **1-800-873-7545** or **1-913-677-3200**.